A Body Less Perfect
My Life's Journey with Cerebral Palsy

My body
Is that which encompasses me.
At times
It attempts to control me.

But make no mistake.
It will never
No, not ever
Define me.

You cannot see me
You cannot feel me
You can only experience me.

I am who I am
I am not what you see.

By
MoorMan

Farolito Press
P.O. Box 60003
Grand Junction, Colorado 81506

Cover Photo was modified from a photo of the author that appeared in the Clarksdale (Mississippi) Press Register Newspaper circa 1961.

ISBN 978-0-9818339-0-3

Table of Contents

The following poems reveal my life growing up and aging with Cerebral Palsy (CP). Some aspects of my life were good; others were not. Many people have gone through similar times; I am not alone on my journey.

My life has been a mixture of bad and good times. Fortunately, there have been more good times than bad. I wish for others a life as blessed as mine.

If, by chance, you know one of the 500,000 or so Americans with CP, share the poems with them. They are the reason I wrote them, especially the young.

A lifelong disability does not have to be a lesser life. I have lived a good life through middle age and look forward to many more happy years.

I have a wonderful wife and daughter and live very close to what most consider a normal life. My career has been successful and I continue to enjoy and have success on a regular basis.

Life is good!

MoorMan

Poetry: attempting to heal one's soul through the thoughtful arrangement of words
MoorMan

Cerebral Palsy is a lifelong condition; we come into this world with it; we leave with it. For the first part of my life, I tried to hide its effect on my body.

Hiding the Obvious

For many years I hid the obvious.
Part of my body was weak and unattractive.
People noticed but tried to ignore it.
My solution?
I tried to hide it.

Some called me a gimp.
Others thought me (somehow) retarded.
It ruled my life; therefore,
I vowed to hide it.

Sports were never an option.
Running, jumping, and catching, in no way easy.
As I made excuses, my mind became my refuge.
It created the perfect escape where,
I could hide it.

Clothing I used to cover the less than perfect.
Long sleeved shirts, no short pants,
I tried to pass these off as stylish.
Behind the fashion veil,
I continued to hide it.

With my quick wit and snappy comebacks,
I kept the cruel at bay.
Their slow wits were my salvation.
Using my intellect,
I continued to hide it.

With age and maturity, I soon discovered,
My imperfections had many companions.
A strong mind would survive and support a weak body.
Besides,
I was never really able to hide it.

My Cerebral Palsy was attributed to the conditions of my birth complicated by my large birth size. I was born in a rural sharecropper's house in Tunica County, Mississippi. The house had neither indoor plumbing nor running water. There are, however, worse places to start.

Three Rooms and a Path

1948 and the December weather is bitter.
The sharecropper's house, diminutive and cold.
A small pregnant woman, scared and in agony.
Rising water and the doctor is late.

Three children in the house, another in the ground.
Swollen belly fits like a well-worn dress.
A new drug helped ease the way.
The baby came too quickly with only one pain.

No running water, no indoor plumbing.
A mother and eleven-pound baby to clean.
The pot bellied stove glowed red hot.
The stars were not aligned.

The baby's skull was fractured.
Only God knows the plan.
An altered life was forged;
The friendship with pain began.

Ignorance helped cloud the dark, early morning sky.
A boy never to be right.
His large size belayed the obvious.
The unusual journey begins.

My first memory is of an occurrence under the front porch of our sharecropper's shack. Hopefully, the Great Spirit overlooked my activity.

First Memory

Small and dark the house appeared to be.
Inside, no wallpaper or paint to be found.
An outside covered with cheap asphalt shingles,
Home was but three rooms and a path.

The front protected by a wide covered porch.
The house built two feet above the ground.
The dwelling,
Home to a struggling sharecropper family.
Protection for husband, wife, and five children.

A family's second youngest,
The only one yet to walk.
Even the baby girl could easily stroll around.
Three older kids helped as they could in the fields.
The little boy, on his bottom, merely scooted about.

The boy was a small frail child.
Doctors recommended he be sent away.
His mother objected.
So under the porch, he often played.

His life's first memory was under the porch one day.
Captured by hand, a small baby chicken.
Tiny hands desperately held on as the bird resisted.
Because his diminutive feathers,
The little boy was busy a pickin'.

When I was five years old, my aunt enticed me to walk using a black doll. Why I was encouraged by such a toy, is unknown. Since the doctors in Memphis had said I would never walk, this came as a big surprise to my family.

The Black Doll

Birth plus five,
A small boy with braces leaned against the wall.
No steps had ever been taken,
His body obviously broken.

Aunt Lena wanted him,
Her brown baby to raise.
It was not to be.

Aunt Lena used the black doll to beckon.
He reached; it was pulled back.

She smiled,
The teasing hand motioned him forward.
The black doll awaited
Give it to me, he pleaded.

Then,
The little boy was stumbling across the floor.
Black doll clutched by his little hand,
His body, not as broken as thought.
Could there be more?

At a young age, I became the March of Dimes Poster Boy for Coahoma County, Mississippi. It was the beginning of my exposure to the media.

Poster Boy

Once upon a time,
In a cotton-pickin' Delta town,
Celebrity happened upon me;
My picture you may have seen.

March of Dimes Poster Boy,
One and me the same.
Chosen for reasons,
I know not why.

Smiling for the camera,
My 15 minutes of fame,
Andy would have been proud of me.

The campaign's image,
A brown broken one.
We all smiled,
Without a clue.

A good thing I suppose,
A small face to raise money.
I personally never financially benefited.
Knowing me now, you realize that's quite funny.

I felt being in the March of Dimes Poster Boy Campaign was slightly dishonest. You see, the March of Dimes Poster Boys all had polio. As you know by now, that was not my condition.

As part of campaign publicity, I was photographed sitting on a rifle held between two National Guard soldiers.

Guilt Money

A Mississippi Delta town,
Time to raise the yearly guilt money.
Let's march out the lame;
Perhaps a few hearts to be claimed.

A smiling mother, a smiling father,
A rifle seat between two soldiers.
Big smile on a small Indian face,
The gun holds more interest than the game.

Roll up his left pant leg;
Make sure the brace can be seen.
Is he looking at the camera?
His photo image we must obtain.

The little boy hasn't a clue,
His cuteness is for sale.
His big brown eyes will bring them calling,
Nickels and dimes in a plastic collection can.

The boy is not impressed with the news,
He remembers only the gun.
The pious citizens remark on the poor crippled boy,
The fund raising campaign has begun.

As a child, life was often cruel. Dealing with taunting classmates was an everyday event. Every once in a while, though, justice raises its head, even for the handicapped among us.

The Bully

The bully pushed him down and ran.
A skinny brown boy lying on the ground.
The bully is back taunting.
Just out of reach,
The boy tries to catch him.

The metal brace makes running,
Slow and painful.
The bully, mocking and cruel,
Skinny boy's chase seems hopeless.
He prays,
Please let me catch him.

Day after day the same,
No help in sight.
All just laugh and point,
Catching the bully is now more than a game.

Teachers feel sorry for the skinny boy,
Stop, they say to the bully, stop.
Leave the boy alone.
Their work is over,
After all,
It's only innocent fun.

The bully is coming to play his sport.
Hiding behind a bush,
The skinny boy holds his breath.
An arm around the surprised throat,
I caught you.
He nearly choked the bully to death.

As a small child, doctors offered many opinions about my condition. Many thought I was mentally challenged. Much of my day was spent sitting on the end of the sofa. Some of my best creativity happened there.

The Sofa

He sat on the end of the sofa,
Alone.
The house small and cluttered,
His mind his companion.
Brothers and sisters,
In the sun.

The woman in the kitchen,
Chattering away.
The playful noises from outside,
Invade.
Running and playing,
But a dream.
His mind,
Races away.

Outside,
The forbidden land awaits.
He'll be hurt,
He cannot go.
Brother makes a face through the window,
He doesn't understand the pain.

Crippled and maybe insane,
Never to be trusted alone.
He won't be here long,
They have all agreed.

Why is he different,
Why can't he be sane?
Braces creak as he moves,
The sofa is his domain.

When I was young, people dining at a restaurant next door to our humble home would throw coins to my brother and me. If you are poor, it really helps to be cute.

Ramon's

Two little boys,
Playing in the gravel.
One short and light, the other,
Dark and tall.
Two brothers sharing the same bed.
One healthy and strong,
One not.

Ramon's in view next door.
A fancy restaurant the boys will never enter.
Big cars and fancy people,
Into the restaurant and out again.
The rich continue to come and go.

The boys' house is simple and plain.
Four rotting rooms perched high above the river.
A hole in the floor,
Where the crippled one fell.
Dry and warm,
But not much more.

A snake in a bureau drawer;
Baby mice in another room found.
It's not much,
But it's home,
To seven people and Brownie the dog.

Big brown eyes stare at the patrons;
Rich eyes look uncomfortably back.
Nickels thrown out the window with guilt,
To the small boys from the shack.

In the second grade, I had two protectors, my brother and the school Principal. My brother occupied his role for many years. The Principal served for only a short time.

Protectors

Two second grade boys.
Eliza Clark their school;
On Mississippi Street, sat their home.
A three-room shotgun house,
Their family's simple dwelling.

Reading was the boys' passion.
All books, in their grade quickly consumed.
A thirst for knowledge ignited.
The flame survived in but one.

Solitary boy with braces limping about.
The Principal, Ms. Carroll, took pity.
At lunch, his tray she carried.
Perhaps a soiled floor, was more her concern.

A small guardian of the lame,
One boy watched over the other.
Many faces met his fist,
Protecting a little brown boy,
With the same name.

Ms. Carroll also fretted and protected.
Her thoughts and actions masked by charm.
She followed and watched, so the crippled one
Would experience no harm.

Because of my earlier experience with doctors, it was later in life before I really learned to trust them, kind of. To this day, I am probably more cautious than most when it comes to medical treatment.

All The Doctors Said

As a child,
I wasn't very active,
Never having crawled.
I scooted around on my bottom,
Finally walking at five.

This boy will never walk,
All the doctors said.
This boy is severely retarded,
All the doctors said.

Put him in an institution,
He will be better off,
The family can't handle him,
All the doctors said.

Medicine is a dark science,
On its grandest day.
Bad doctors guess,
The good ones diagnose.

My experience with doctors,
Is mixed at best.
Some have been extraordinary,
Others barely passed their final test.

When I was very young, we left the cotton fields of the plantation behind. We moved to the closest town and settled in on the wrong side of the tracks. Life for us was getting better.

House on Mississippi Street

A house,
Brown grass in the yard.
Called a shotgun,
Its shape long and narrow.
Rooms limited to three,
A sleeping bed in each.

Five children,
Two struggling parents.
The fight to survive,
Unending.
A sharecropper's shack,
Still a memory.
Indoor plumbing,
Yesterday unknown,
Today a treat.

Four children in the yard playing,
One sadly observing life,
As it passes by the window.
Existence not really bad,
Yesterday was worse.

Tomorrow there is hope,
The town offers more chances.
A little boy's life is evolving,
His future,
In other's hands.

Cotton fields traded for asphalt.
Scooting,
Becomes a stumbled dance.
Big brown eyes searching.
Will life really give him a chance?

I was raised in a racially bigoted society. As I grew, I discovered that bigotry often extended to people with different physical abilities. Bigotry is merely the manifestation of fear, fear of the different.

Two Brothers the Same

Bigots are made,
Not born.
Children use words taught;
Adults use words they believe.
The crippled boy was taught,
but he never believed.
Black people are different; respect the distinction.
We are not the same.
Friendship with them will destroy our race.

Different also,
Are the crippled.
Lame boy and you,
Never the same.
At his hand,
Others will stare.
Crude expressions,
His joke of the day.

Black or crippled,
Two brothers the same.
Shared by each,
Socially induced pain.
One because of color;
The other,
Physical shame.

Black or crippled, both are objects of scorn.
With either,
Association not allowed.
For both,
Bigotry and name calling the same.
For the crippled, however,
Color is not to blame.

Everyone loves a new baby. When the baby is revealed to be less than perfect, however, adoration begins a long journey toward fear.

Adoration Misplaced

New baby,
Loved and adored.
So perfect,
His brown hands and feet,
Eyes, black and shiny,
Hair, dark as coal.

Days later,
Crying never stops.
Behavior like this never seen.
Defects,
Not perceived.

Diagnosis, he's crippled,
Brain not the same.
Adoration, joined by pity, still maintained.
A baby after all, yet,
Hard to explain.

Young teenager,
Handicap a blight.
He's crippled,
What a pity.
Keep him from my view;
Fear him I now do.

A young man,
All defects on display.
Can't you make him disappear?
Fear turned to fright;
What if _my_ child should so appear?

Some people say Bulldogs have a special sense when it comes to children in need. I have believed that theory since childhood.

Bulldog

A bulldog,
From nowhere he came.
His owners unknown.
The big old body,
Slow and lame.
Many dog years,
He had seen.

A species,
Known for its power.
The bulldog detects my need.
A small boy alone,
The dog comes,
To stay by me.

My companion he became.
Both slow of motion,
Me before my time,
He by nature's decline.

Some say a bulldog is special,
This dog friend of mine.
He detected my mental need,
The help of silence,
I then freely received.

I never knew,
From whence he came.
One day,
He simply did not show.
Helped through my childhood crisis,
My bulldog friend knew,
It was time to go.

Nigra is what many polite southern white people used to call blacks instead of using the ugly "N" word. The way it was said often sounded just as offensive.

Nigra in the Park

A little boy, playing in the park.
His big brown eyes brightly shining.
The brace on his leg, squeaking.
His brown sun-baked skin,
Darker than any.

The others ran away and left him.
With his CP, it was impossible to keep up.
He didn't care though,
The day was sunny,
Freedom, the invisible companion at his side.

The little boy didn't think of color.
The sun pulling his Indian heritage forth.
How could he know,
Others thought him different?

Silently, he played alone.

The white lady saw him,
Limping their way.
Her children,
All playing together.
The little boy,
Hoping to join in.

She hastened to step between;
Her cold hard look glaring.
Nigras aren't allowed in the park.

Without a doubt,
She was addressing him.
He knew he was brown,
But was he really that dark?

Twice each year I traveled to Memphis for an examination. Crippled children from three states were herded into the Baptist Hospital basement waiting their turns. Each visit my mother heard the same prognosis.

The Basement

Twice a year the Greyhound bus we rode.
A Memphis Hospital was our destination.
A long, narrow, dingy basement,
Rewarded our arrival.
Mama must have been scared,
I thought it quite the adventure.

Crippled children gathered,
Contiguous states blended.
Doctors hurried to serve for free.
A hundred broken bodies,
With anxious mothers waited.

An endless line of metal folding chairs became,
Our handicap of the day.
Overhead pipes, our clouds in the sky.
A dirty floor, our playground.

Many children cried and screamed;
My silence,
Deafening to those around me.

His grades, how bad are they?
Severely mentally retarded,
They assumed I must be.

I would not live much longer,
Mama was always told.
A crippled boy like me,
No real future you see.

Before my first surgery, I met a small girl with much more difficulty than me. For a time, we shared fear, then once again we were on our own.

Fear Shared

It was the night before surgery,
Scared I had to be.
What would it be like,
When they took the knife to me?

I was in a small lobby,
Watching TV.
She sat in her robe
Watching me.

Two young children,
Sharing common space.
Looking at each other,
Sharing TV.

She came beside me,
I said hello.
She sat down,
Sharing her fear with me.

I was having foot surgery,
She was being cut into her brain.
I survived to adulthood.
For her,
I cannot say the same.

My first real experience with death happened when my hospital roommate died. I knew it was sad, but was too young to really understand. Since then, I have learned its true meaning.

Empty Bed

I was a small boy of 11,
He a teenager about 16.
We shared a hospital room together;
Two boys side by side,
Together for the moment.

I was in great pain,
His suffering was almost over.
My foot had started to curl under,
His body was struggling in vain.

I had one surgery on my foot,
Then another.
He merely lay there with drugs,
Entering his veins.
My foot swelled in the cast,
So I complained.

Probably in pain,
He never protested.
His visitors were few.
My mother sleeping on a cot by my side,
We three,
Enduring the long nights together.

The surgeon's knife caused my pain.
He was very sick,
But with no one to blame.
He died before I went home.
I never even knew his name.

I spent the better part of a year in the Shriners Crippled Children's Hospital in Memphis, Tennessee. The hospital had manicured grounds and a beautiful garden. It was truly a beautiful place for housing so much pain.

Life in Shriners Hospital

The grounds were beautiful;
Shrubs, flowers, and trees abound.
A wheelchair ride outside,
Joy to a boy away from home.

Inside the building,
A bedroom home to twenty.
All manner of boys together,
Loneliness endured as one.

Girls in their own ward,
Giggling when boys were near.
Budding hormones on display,
Boys too naive to notice.

Babies in their own special place,
Names written on cribs.
No mothers to cuddle,
Only orderlies to care.

All in all,
Not a bad place.
The little brown boy has lived in worse.
His mind becomes his refuge.
His physical place,
Merely a temporary curse.

There was a school in the hospital where all ambulatory patients had to go. It was nice to be normal for a change. As a matter of fact, I felt more normal there, at that time, than I ever have since.

Shriners School

Ms. Gray was our teacher.
On metal crutches,
She walked each day.
Hair color,
Mirrored her name.
Her teaching style,
Kind and patient.

Six of us students,
Bedridden not allowed to participate.
Grade levels several,
Instruction pretty much the same.

This school I enjoyed,
We were all the same.
Not a healthy body among us,
Nor a strong one to stare,
And be profane.

We were there but temporarily,
Grades never used to separate.
The smart and challenged,
Equally treated.
Mainstreaming at its best.

French the subject I remember.
Gum, Ms. Gray said,
I wasn't allowed to chew.
It prevented enunciation you see;
With it,
I could not parlez vous.

Every Saturday night at the hospital was movie night. Not until I was grown, with a family of my own, did I understand the sacrifice made by the Shriners.

Shriners' Saturday Nights

It must be Saturday night;
The Shriners are here again.
Their own families left behind,
Personal time,
Dedicated to us.
Who are these men,
In funny hats?

All patients moved to the big room.
Those who can walk,
Move themselves.
Some children are in body casts,
Space-bound to beds.
Their tiny worlds,
Rolled in with the rest.

A popcorn machine is doing its thing.
The buttery smell brings back memories;
Oh, to be,
In the Paramount Theater back home.
Maybe my brothers and sisters,
Are there thinking of me.

The movie projector is being set up;
Two large reels to entertain.
A scratchy noise our segue,
The screen lights up.

The men laugh and joke,
To them this is great fun.
For us crippled kids,
Our weekly entertainment.
The flickering bulb,
Brighter than the sun.

One lazy Sunday afternoon, the movie star, Dale Robertson, wandered into the hospital with a starlet on each arm. His generosity was accompanied by a total lack of photographers or fanfare - a good man doing a good deed.

Dale Robertson

Sunday afternoon,
Weekly visitation long over.
Boys hanging around the ward,
Looking bored with little to do.
If only something would happen.

There's a lot of noise,
Coming from the hallway;
A commotion is about to brew.
Someone or something is out there;
We wish we only knew who.

Suddenly through our door,
A huge cowboy appears.
Who is this guy,
But more important, who are the other two?

It's the famous cowboy,
From on the TV.
He just dropped by,
To say hello.
With a beautiful blonde on each arm,
What a sight is he.

Dale Robertson was his name.
We'd all seen him,
In *Tales of Wells Fargo,*
On TV.
Why had he come to see us cripple children?
Getting an answer to our question,
Was never to be.

One day at the Shriners Crippled Children's Hospital, a group of rich women appeared. Condescension was the only thing thicker than their perfume. Even though young, it just felt wrong to me. I learned early how it felt to be pitied; I have never liked it.

Good Ladies From Town

The good ladies from town,
Came calling today.
With their fake smiles and fancy ways,
I could sense condescension,
All around.

One hovered over my bed.
Oh, what a cute little brown boy.
With a silky voice and pursed lips,
She asked,
"What's wrong with you?"

I tried to answer,
As any polite boy should.
They operated on my leg,
Now I must learn to walk again.
I answered,
As her eyes went darting around.

The ladies were on a holy mission,
You see.
Poor little crippled kids to tend.
Oh,
What a story it would make,
Telling those at the country club,
Over cocktails tonight.

"I helped this cute little poor boy today.
He was shy,
Didn't say a lot.
I gave him a flashlight,
He was, after all,
A pathetic little tot."

I had the unique opportunity to meet Richard Nixon, when he was running against John Kennedy for President. Regardless of what happened to him later, I have always had a warm spot in my heart for the man.

Meeting V.P. Nixon

Crippled students, a Shriners' station wagon full.
Handicapped teacher along to guide us.

Downtown Memphis, our historic destination.
A political parade, the educational goal.

We sat parked, staring back along the route.
Those who could sat on the hood.

Secret service agents, stationed all about.
What an exciting time to live,
my friends, teacher, and me.

Vice President Nixon, coming down the street.
Police on motorcycles leading the way.

Our car parked in his direct path.
Labeled "Crippled Children," for all to see.

He points at our small congregation,
With a word, the parade is halted.
With a smile and a wave, he exits the big open car.
I am the first he sees.

With a big grin, he offers his hand.
A writing pen, his gift to me.
I feel seven feet tall, even though,
I cannot stand.

Living in the Shriners Hospital was like living in a small town. Boys fought, little girls had crushes, and life went on.

Chariots in Flight

The two boys were having angry words today.
Both in wheelchairs out on the balcony,
Choosing to fight.
Two crippled boys,
Doing what comes naturally.

Wheelchairs rolling toward each other,
Their version of Roman chariots in flight.
Chairs sped into each others,
Little fists struck out.

No real harm could be done,
Wheelchairs kept them far apart.
But boys will be boys,
Continuing their fearsome fight.

As with most such battles,
Duration was brief.
Fighting over arms of big wooden wheelchairs,
Quickly brought on fatigue.

The fight was finished;
Temporary violence ends.
Boys smile at each other and shake hands.
Now it's over,
Once again they can be friends.

At the Shriners Hospital, parents could visit for one hour a week; no other visitation allowed. Any type of food brought had to be shared with all other children.

Affection A Rationed Thing

Sunday,
But one visitation day.
An hour after lunch allowed.
Parents only, no others permitted.
Family,
Not much appreciated at Shriners.

Treats arriving during visitation hour,
Socialism ruled the day.
Whatever was brought to the hospital,
Shared by all.

Candy,
We tried to hide.
A bar did not go far.
A cake could never be saved,
For supper it must be divided.

A small toy often provided.
Mama's way of showing love.
A hug and a kiss in passing,
Affection, a rationed thing.

Any charity hospital is prone to cash shortages. Shriners was no different. I remember one night when food was running short. The staff carried on as best they could.

No Food Tonight

Supper time at Shriners Crippled Children's Hospital.
In the dining room,
All ambulatory gathered.
Sunday night,
The week is almost over.
Monday,
Just another day.

Food,
Never great,
But at least on time.
Not tonight, however,
Something must be broken.

Crippled children,
Chatter while they wait.
The food must surely be on its way.
We're all so hungry;
Why must we wait?

The food is finally served,
Two canned biscuits per child.
On each table sits a small jar of jam,
Supper dished right from the pans.

The hospital is out of food,
No other supper can be prepared.
Meat and vegetables are all gone,
It's almost as if no one really cared.

When I was in the Shriners Crippled Children's Hospital, my parents came to see me at every opportunity. Other children were not as lucky; their parents never came.

Forgotten Children

The Shriners Hospital, for a time was my home.
My siblings,
Crippled children the same.
We shared a ward together;
Together, we shared our pain.

My fate more just,
Parents who visited on each occasion.
Loving grandparents who thought of me at night,
A concerned cousin who continued to write.

Many in the ward,
Lucky like me.
Visits on Sunday always the best,
Their parents forever caring,
Families hoping they would,
Somehow be blessed.

Others in the ward,
Not so lucky.
Abandoned by parents,
Who did not care.
Families but a faint memory,
Sunday visitations,
A bitter reminder.

They were,
But accidents of nature.
Handicaps,
Too horrible to view.
Parents ashamed of them,
Being loved,
Something they never knew.

Next door to the Shriners Hospital was a hospital for adults with disabling conditions. Many nights were spent speculating about them. Many nights were also spent listening to them.

Adult Hospital Next Door

The Shriners Hospital,
A place for crippled children.
The hospital next door,
Not quite the same.
Patients there,
A very different type.
Ones who would,
Never go home.

At night, cries in the air.
Like a building full of caged animals,
They wailed all night.
Their only peace,
During the day.

Who they were, we never really knew.
Some said they were crazy,
A story that rung true.

I felt sorry for such sad people.
Who had destined them to such a horrible place?
What could possibly be their crimes,
Warranting such grief?

Impossible to know the truth.
A small boy trying to judge,
from the comfort of his bed.
Even though they went on living, they would probably,
Have been better off dead.

Before leg waxing was popular, I received the spa treatment every day. I would repeatedly immerse my left foot and ankle in hot wax until they were covered by many layers. Guess what, as a permanent hair removal system, it worked.

Leg Waxing

Recovering from surgery was never easy.
What they did to me, might make some queasy.
Shortly after I was cut out of the cast,
A physical therapist commenced her task.

Once a day, to the therapy room I went.
Some kids screaming, from having their bodies bent.
My luck was very strong I would say,
My body never required contortions in that way.

My personal torture was of a different kind.
To tell the truth, I didn't really mind.
Into hot wax, my foot and ankle they would dip.
After hardening, off my leg, the wax,
They would rip.

Daily, the ritual was repeated, several times in a row.
Hopefully, stronger my foot and ankle would grow.
Boredom was my companion as I sat on a stool,
Waiting for my next immersion, in the hot waxy pool.

All these years later, I still remember the hot paraffin.
Applied again and again to my tender skin.

All my leg hair, it did rip away.
And it has never come back, not even to this day.

After three surgeries on my left foot and leg, there was concern that I would never walk again. It wasn't easy, but I finally persevered.

He'll Never Walk Again

On my crippled body, number of surgeries three.
A growing club foot, my source of pain you see.

The pride of successful surgery heard in their talk.
Now their next concern, would I ever again walk.

At the kitchen table, mother sat drinking a Coke.
Conversation with Aunt Pearl, anything but a joke.

She was very concerned, it was in her tone of talking.
There was a problem, I was no longer walking.

Their medical magic had been worked on me,
But as to walking, all were waiting to see.

I rolled around the house in a wheelchair,
Wooden crutches, I often used a pair.

Mama and Pearl's talk, from the next room I heard.
All their fear manifested in each word.

Could what they were saying really be true,
Was walking an activity with which I was through?

I determined that day, their opinion would not stand.
On my body, I would make more of a demand.

It wasn't long after all the talking,
That once again, I was practicing my walking.

All of my life has been challenged by a left hand that does not function well. As with most such situations, the right has overdeveloped so as to compensate.

Hands Not The Same

I have two hands,
As does most everyone else.
One is marginally functional;
The other is something else.

My right hand is talented,
In all things hands are designed to do.
It can flip a coin;
Catching a ball is easy to perform.
If it can be done,
The right hand will succeed.

My left hand is a different story;
It refuses orders from the brain.
No task is easy for it to do;
At nothing does it excel.

The left hand spasms at night;
It seems to want something to do.
I put it under my pillow;
The weight of my head calming it.

The eye on my left is dominant.
So, left-handed,
My body was designed to be.
Nature had a different plan though;
A brain injury, left me with CP.

The skill level in my hands is polarized. The left requires a great deal of concentration to accomplish the simplest of tasks. Such has been the case my entire life.

Gentle Hand

My body possesses two very different hands,
One is skilled in all things;
The other wilted.
They should be the same,
But will never be.

One with the strength of overuse,
The other weakened by inactivity.
Attached to the same brain,
But noticeably very different.

Over their life,
My right hand has known violence.
The left never anything but tame,

My left hand is gentle,
My right cannot make the same claim.
How can one hand be so good,
And its mate not be the same?

Most handicapped children know the embarrassment and hurt of schoolyard sports. When we would be chosen, was never a mystery.

Last Picked

Recess brought the boys running;
One ran slower than all the rest.
It was football season,
An emotional chill in the air.

A football,
Being tossed about.
A game in the air,
Time to choose up sides.
The slow one,
Not really liking the sport.

Loser, preordained.
Never the team with the least points,
No, that would never be.
It would be,
The child picked last.

Boys stood anxiously by.
Two bigger ones,
Would captains be.
Cruel choosing started,
Time to be shamed again.

First, the strong ones,
Next, all those who could run fast.
Finally the fat ones,
The crippled boy was always chosen last.

My grandmother looked as if she had been sent over by central casting for the part of an Indian grandmother. Not only was she very loving, she also had a gift for healing. I still miss her to this day.

Warts

My grandma was an Indian lady by birth.
I loved her dearly;
She was truly the salt of the earth.
In the summer,
Junior and I would go for a stay.
Whatever we wanted,
She usually let us have our way.
She and grandpa ran a small service station.
A perfect environment for two small boys on vacation.
Each day we would play,
Around the big gas tanks.
Our mischievous ways usually resulted,
In unsafe pranks.
I remember one summer,
I had nine warts on my hand.
Grandma told me,
Such a condition could never stand.
She told me she had an Indian cure.
I believed,
Because of my faith in her,
I was mighty sure.
A wooden match she struck, so it would burn.
After a few seconds, she blew it out,
As was its turn.
On my warts,
She rubbed the match's burnt soot.
Then under the porch,
She buried it deep, about a foot.
In a few days,
My warts were all gone.
My hand with the warts,
Was now smooth as a stone.
My grandma was an Indian healer of sorts,
Lucky for me, her specialty just happened to be warts.

When I was a small child, the doctors decided I should wear braces 24 hours a day. I haven't had a decent night's sleep since.

Sleeping in Braces

Metal leg braces,
I wore many years,
Correction was the intended thing.
Days were not so bad,
The pain visited mainly at night.

Braces and two siblings,
My bedmates.
Comfortable nights rare,
A sibling on each side,
Braces on my left foot in the covers below.

Children grow at night,
It seems.
Bones and ligaments increase.
Foot grows crooked in the dark,
Restricted, it has to be.

High topped brown shoe,
Braces attached to each side.
Leather strap around the top,
The shoe's toe cut out.

Braced shoe for daytime,
More metal adorned my shoe at night.
Never slept the darkness through,
Nights of sleeplessness began because of that shoe.

For any person with a physical disability, recess and being exposed to a lot of kids running and jumping isn't always fun. I tried to avoid that form of social interaction whenever possible.

Recess

Recess was never fun for me,
Running kids not a treat.
Often I stayed inside,
Satisfied to be alone.

Running was difficult,
Often painful for me.
Playing with the others,
Also painful,
But not physically.

Sometimes staying inside,
I was not alone.
A little girl I knew,
Sat inside with me.

Why she was there,
I never knew.
Being sick,
Not an excuse.
Maybe she just,
Wanted to be.

I enjoyed her company.
Her reasoning,
Not my goal to discover.
Why she stayed inside with me,
Maybe,
She was just allowing her kindness to run free.

My mother tried to protect me at all cost. She knew, however, that she could not always be around. Teach a boy to fish and he'll never be hungry; teach him self-defense and he'll never be picked on.

The Knife

When I was about eight, I went to the park,
Often staying until after dark.
On my left leg, I wore a metal brace.
It was attached to a leather shoe that,
up my leg did lace.

Its weight precluded me being swift on the run.
Consequently, the park was not always fun.
Other children would tease and not let me play,
All I could do was try to run away.

Sometimes, the bigger kids, tried to do me bodily harm.
There was no appeasing them, even with my charm.
They would push and knock me down,
All I could do was lay in the dirt with a frown.

My mother tired, of their rude behavior,
Had decided, I needed a savior.
Her forehead wrinkled in thought,
She decided the big kids, needed to be fought.

Mama gave me a knife with a sharp blade.
She said it would help me not be afraid.
Mama said, cut them if they bother you.
Once the boys saw the knife, my troubles were through.

Some things we take for granted, like shoes. I remember my first pair without braces attached. What an exciting time.

Regular Shoes

From early in life, braces I wore on my feet.
Soon discarding the ones on my right, ooh how sweet.
The left ones, however, I wore for many years.
The pain of walking, often brought me to tears.

The braces were steel, the shoe heavy leather.
The weight of the two were cumbersome together.
It wasn't bad when I was young, just learning to talk.
After all, it would be years before I could actually walk.

But walking with them was a major chore.
Who wants to drag a heavy brace across the floor?
At first, I would hold on to something and give it a try,
Determined, I would never let them see me cry.

Ultimately, surgery improved my gait,
But in the braces, I continued to wait.
I hated to wear my heavy brown shoes,
Even the thought of it, gave me the blues.

One day the word came,
No longer did my shoes need to be the same.
What a momentous day containing such glorious news.
For the first time in my life, I could wear regular shoes.

Skating was yet another athletic endeavor at which I failed. Balance has never been my strong suit. Balancing with wheels tied to my feet proved almost impossible.

Learning to Skate

Skating was a thing many kids liked to do,
My brothers and sisters were very good.
They would race quickly forward,
Backward they could skate too.

Managing a skating rink,
my grandpa endeavored to do.
Located in the country, it was Saturday night fun.
Just a great big room is all it was.
Oh, but what a gorgeous wooden floor,
running through.

A two bedroom apartment tacked on the back.
The grand folks did their living there.
Not much to brag about,
But love it never lacked.

I tried to skate on the big wooden rink.
Because of my feet,
Girl's high-top skates I had to wear.
Poor balance made others laugh at me, I think.

Pulling me round and round the polished floor,
The rail became my partner.
I turned loose after awhile,
Only to end up very sore.

Skating and CP,
Together, not meant to be.
The next wheels in my future,
On a chair would be.

For handicapped children, there is no greater horror than gym class with "normal" kids. It was never to be enjoyed; it was merely to be survived. Junior is my brother.

Coming in Last

Gym class was an activity I never embraced.
An equal opportunity,
Never would it be.
Generously kind to the physically adept,
A horror for people challenged like me.

Jumping on the trampoline,
I could never successfully do.
Doing pull-ups, a 50% effort at best.
One strong arm,
Never enough to pass the test.

But most hated of all,
Running around the track.
The fat guys and me,
Always came in last.
Such an outcome always destined to be.

A physical fitness test in progress,
Student teams picked alphabetically.
Junior, several others and me.
The fastest and slowest in one group,
Truly a sight to see.

The swiftest in the class,
Slowing to help me.
Coach grew angry and shouted.
He expected me to come in last,
But of Junior, his speed the coach had always touted.

As with many physical skills, I learned swimming later in life. It was all due to a kind boy who, no doubt, grew into a kind man.

Learning to Swim

Charlie and I were classmates,
Big and gregarious was he.
Life-guarding was his job,
Guarding swimmers' valuables was me.

Charlie asked, isn't it a shame?
Water all aroun',
Kid working at the swimming pool,
Not knowing how to swim; he'll probably drown?

When I just smiled,
He said he'd teach me.
How hard could it really be?
Hard, he was destined to see.

My body reacted differently.
Charlie soon learned to his dismay.
Therefore the swimming crawl, I could never do,
No, not at all, even if we practiced day after day.

Not one to give up,
Charlie taught me to float.
Then he taught me to swim on my right side.
About that time, he started to gloat.

Throughout my life, I have lived without fine-finger dexterity in my left hand. I simply became skilled at improvising. What one cannot do, one learns to do without.

Dexterity

Fine-finger dexterity,
Not my left hand's gift.
Ability to button the front of my shirt,
never in an attempt,
Would my left hand, I lift.

Fifteen before I could button my right cuff.
Hours of practice is what it took.
Willing the fingers to obey the brain,
Many days I tried, until the hand shook.

A simple thing, to off the floor,
Retrieve a dime.
Sometimes I can do it,
But never consistently, never time after time.

To use a fork,
In my left hand,
Never a good thing to try
Difficult for many to understand.

The hand to me is fine.
It serves in its own way.
You'll never hear me complain,
It's mine and hopefully, here to stay.

During my life, I have been through all manner of doctor ordered exercise. Newspaper wadding was not the most onerous. If I had read the papers prior to the wadding, perhaps the whole thing would have been more educational.

Wadding Up Bad News

My left hand is what some call withered.
Turning it down and inward, I hold it funny.
Many feel sorry for me,
My outlook, however, is always sunny.

Doctors perplexed, limb physically normal,
Brain causes a problem with hand.
Bad signals it sends.
Healing, difficult to understand.

Exercise seemed to be the answer,
The hand would get stronger.
Take a newspaper and exercise it,
The hand will strengthen, if you do it longer.

Every night wad up ten newspaper sheets.
The hand will become of more use, you will see.
Keep up the effort night after night,
And the hand will become healthy.

I wadded more newspaper,
More than the average can read.
They became my nightly playthings.
I wadded up newspaper until my hand fatigued.

Learning to ride a bike is a rite of passage for most children. I never learned to ride a two-wheeled bike; therefore, I always felt something was missing. It was replaced by shame.

My Horrible Secret

Everyone could ride a bike,
Even the crippled kids I knew.
But not me,
Balancing a bike was not to be.

I tried when I was little,
To master the metal monster.
But instead,
It seemed to master me.

Embarrassment was my response,
To the weakness perceived.
What if other kids found out,
I could not such a simple thing do?

For most of my life,
I hid this horrible thing.
Not mastering the bike,
Too terrible to believe.

Then it dawned on me,
No one really cared.
So my horrible secret,
I then freely shared.

I grew up in Clarksdale, Mississippi, but for the past 27 years have called Colorado home. Coahoma Street is a fiction novel I wrote about growing up in the 60's.

Looking Back

Mississippi I once called home;
Tunica County the place of my birth.
Clarksdale creating the heart of my youth.
But my real home, was always somewhere else.

Coahoma Street has become my legacy;
The 60's were my baptismal rite.
Racism I never fully embraced;
It seemed more economic, than black and white.

I partook of intolerance as was taught,
But my teenaged years caused doubt.
If we were so different, why were we so alike?
Black and white seemed merely,
Different sides of the same coin.

Today, an older man,
I cannot help but look back.
Was Mississippi ever my home?
I harbor some serious doubts.

My current address is high in the clouds.
I now view Mississippi
through bright blue filtered light.
Coahoma Street encourages me not to go back.
But, does it really matter?
My real home
was always somewhere else.

Printed in the United States
204965BV00001B/1-78/P

9 780981 833903